> If everything around you seems dark,
> look again. You may be the light.
>
> RUMI

Photo by Steve Piepmeier

Sacred Places

Words of Wisdom for Living on Earth

Cheryl McLean

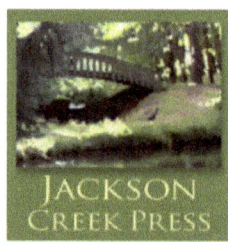

Jackson Creek Press
Corvallis, Oregon
jacksoncreekpress.com

ISBN 978-0-943097-33-6

Library of Congress Control Number: 2023933870

Copyright © 2023 All rights reserved

Designed with love by Cheryl McLean

Dedicated to the many incredible souls who have touched my life with generosity and grace, with love and friendship.

I am grateful for you.

I've been collecting quotes for years—words from people much wiser than I whose messages moved me deeply enough to want to write them down, keep them close. Their words provide solace, as do my rambles in the forest where I live or along the Oregon coast, where my family enjoyed many visits regardless of the weather, or floating on a river or lake in a kayak or canoe. Like the quotes, time spent outdoors has touched and healed places deep within me.

At first I intended this book as a gift for family and friends with the hope that they, too, would find solace within its pages. With the encouragement of their appreciation and several requests for more copies to give their friends, I now want these words and images to have a wider offering.

"You know, green is healing," my dad used to say. I recall a camping trip long ago to Yellowstone National Park. He and I stood within a stand of tall aspen trees. Looking up at the cathedral-like canopy of vibrant green leaves, Dad said, "This is my church. I go to church on Sundays to remember to say 'Thank you.'"

May you find words here that resonate, that touch you as they have me, and images that connect to your own memories of time in Nature's wonders.

Adopt the pace of Nature.

Her secret is patience.

RALPH WALDO EMERSON

Everything flourishes in the nourishment
of appreciation—plants, people, the Earth, moments.
When we live with that appreciation,
we flourish.

Kristi Nelson

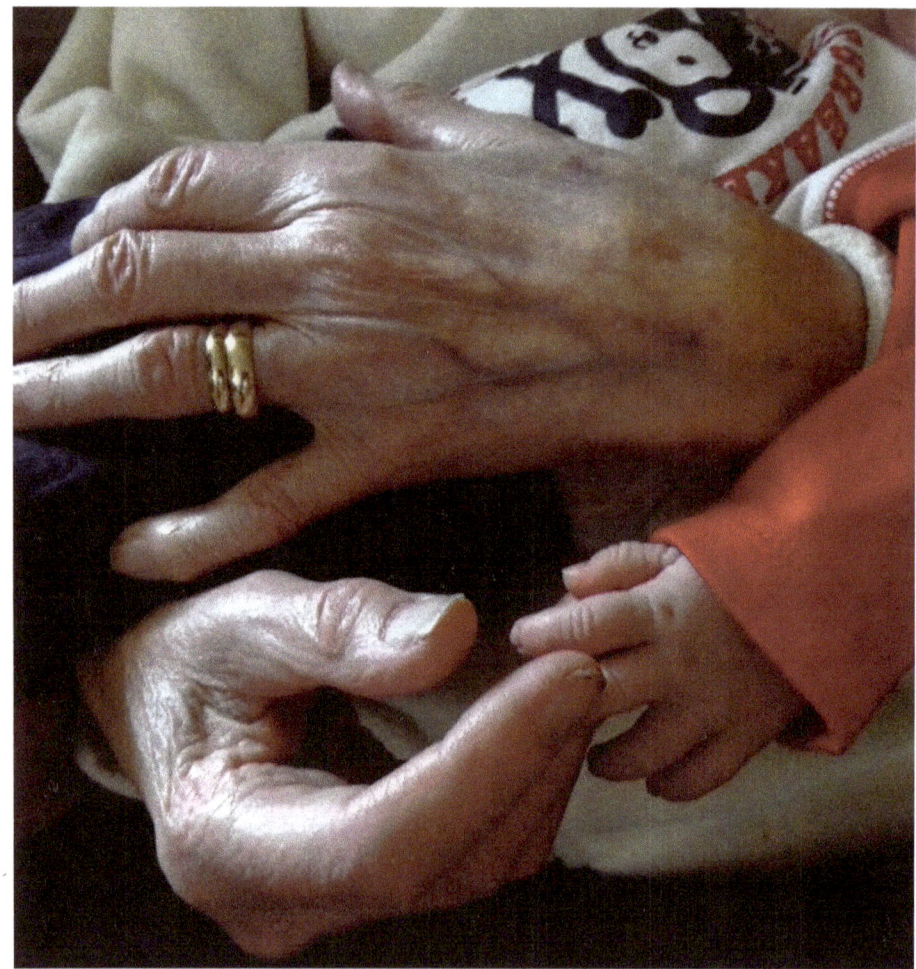

My mother's hands hold her great-grandson Enzo, born about six months before she passed.

Photo by Marilyn McDonald

Often when you think you're at the end of something,
you're at the beginning of something else.

FRED ROGERS

It is spring again.

The earth is like a child

who knows poems by heart.

RAINER MARIA RILKE

Photo by Suzy Conway

Pay attention. Be astonished.

Tell about it.

MARY OLIVER

Even the darkest night
will end and the sun will rise.

VICTOR HUGO

There must be something strangely sacred about salt.
It is in our tears and in the sea.

KHALIL GIBRAN

Find the stillness of eternity within you—
the magic of pure being. And from within that
eternity, notice a tiny spark of joy rising up.

BIRGIT PENZENSTADLER

Life is your art. An open, aware heart is your camera.
A oneness with your world is your film.

ANSEL ADAMS

Perhaps if people talked less,
animals would talk more.

E. B. WHITE

Remember the plants, trees, animal life who all have
their families, their histories too.
Talk to them, listen to them.
They are alive poems.

JOY HARJO

Practice kindness all day to everybody

and you will realize

you're already in heaven now.

JACK KEROUAC

Never lose a holy curiosity.

ALBERT EINSTEIN

The wonder is that we can see these trees

and not wonder more.

Ralph Waldo Emerson

To be astonished is one of the surest ways

of not growing old too quickly.

Sidonie-Gabrielle Colette

The earth is a living thing.

Mountains speak, trees sing,

lakes can think, pebbles have a soul,

rocks have power.

HENRY CROW DOG

I want to be like water.

I want to slip through fingers,

but hold up a ship.

MICHELLE WILLIAMS

Weeds are flowers too,
once you get to know them.

WINNIE THE POOH

You are a speck of stardust
that belonged to universal love.
The blood and the bones in you
are the framework
for galaxies to float in.

RANJITH VALLATHOL

May you learn to dwell
Below the surface of the days
At home with the ebb and flow of
Your own heart's tides.

TRACY SHAW

Trees are sanctuaries.
Whoever knows how to listen to them
can learn the truth.

Hermann Hesse

As I walked the shore on my birthday a few months after Mom's death, I was thinking of her and her love of beach combing when a wave washed over my feet and dropped this gift.

You are walking this life.
Make sure you leave beautiful steps behind.

MORNE PRETORIUS

Big things are often just small things

that are noticed.

MARKUS ZUSAK

Earth carves canyons into rock with nothing more
than a steadfast stream.
Somehow we keep forgetting
that human nature is but a fractal of nature itself.

MARIA POPOVA

There is no end. There is no beginning.
There is only the infinite passion of life.

FEDERICO FELLINI

Let nothing dim the light
that shines from within.

Maya Angelou

Whether you know it or not,
you are the infinite potential
of love, peace, and joy.

AMIT RAY

Photo by Suzy Conway

When life feels too big to handle, go outside.
Everything looks smaller
when you're standing under the sky.

R. L. Knost

Photo by Suzy Conway

Even the smallest shift in perspective
can bring about the greatest healing.

JOSHUA KAI

Wisdom is knowing

what to do next.

DAVID STARR JORDAN

Walk as if you are kissing the Earth

with your feet.

THICH NHAT HAHN

The river that flows in you

also flows in me.

KABIR

Flow like water today.

Bloom like a flower today.

Allow yourself to just be.

RANJITH VALLATHOL

There is no path to happiness.
Happiness is the path.

BUDDHA

We're all just walking each other home.

RAM DAS

FINIS

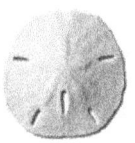

FOR MORE WORDS OF WISDOM

www.ingramcontent.com/pod-product-compliance
Lightning Source LLC
Chambersburg PA
CBHW061821290426
44110CB00027B/2942